from SEA TO SHINING SEA

OKLAHOMA

By Dennis Brindell Fradin and Judith Bloom Fradin

CONSULTANTS
Norbert R. Mahnken, Ph. D., Emeritus Professor of History,
Oklahoma State University, Stillwater

Robert L. Hillerich, Ph.D., Professor Emeritus, Bowling Green State University;
Consultant, Pinellas County Schools, Florida

CHILDREN'S PRESS
A Division of Grolier Publishing
Sherman Turnpike
Danbury, Connecticut 06816

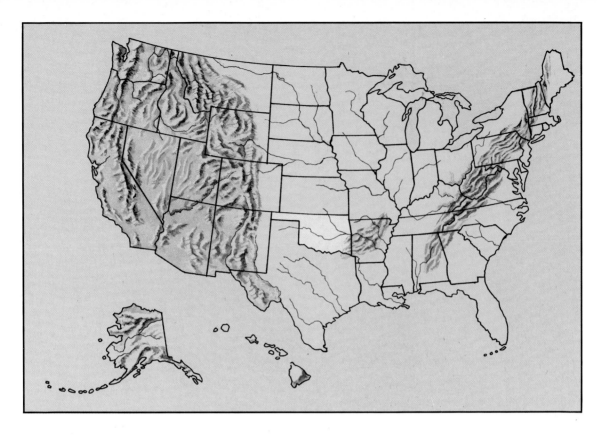

Oklahoma is one of the four states in the region called the Southwest. The other southwestern states are Arizona, New Mexico, and Texas.

For our friend, Charlene Roth, with love

For his help, the authors thank Edward Connie Shoemaker, Director, Library Resources Division, Oklahoma Historical Society

Front cover picture: Myriad Gardens, Oklahoma City; page 1: Wichita Mountains National Wildlife Refuge; back cover: Rock forms on the plains, Black Kettle National Grasslands.

Project Editor: Joan Downing
Design Director: Karen Kohn
Research Assistant: Anthony Fradin
Typesetting: Graphic Connections, Inc.
Engraving: Liberty Photoengraving

Library of Congress Cataloging-in-Publication Data

Fradin, Dennis B.
  Oklahoma / by Dennis Brindell Fradin & Judith Bloom Fradin.
    p.   cm. — (From sea to shining sea)
  Includes index.
  ISBN 0-516-03836-2
    1. Oklahoma—Juvenile literature. [1. Oklahoma.]
I. Fradin, Judith Bloom. II. Title. III. Series: Fradin, Dennis B. From sea to shining sea.
F694.3.F68   1995   94-35023
976.6—dc20   CIP
                                                 AC

Table of Contents

Flight of Spirit, *a mural by Mike Larsen in the rotunda of the state capitol, honors five Oklahoma Indian ballerinas.*

Introducing the Sooner State

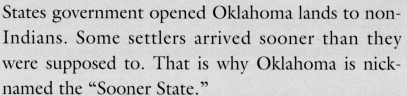

Oklahoma is a state in the southwestern United States. Its name means "red people" in the Choctaw Indian language. American Indians played a big role in Oklahoma's past. So did pioneers. In 1889, the United States government opened Oklahoma lands to non-Indians. Some settlers arrived sooner than they were supposed to. That is why Oklahoma is nicknamed the "Sooner State."

Today, Oklahomans are leaders in mining oil and natural gas. Many Oklahomans make parts of airplanes and rockets. Oklahomans are also noted for growing wheat and for raising beef cattle and horses.

Oklahoma is special in other ways. In what state did the first woman become mayor of a city with more than 200,000 people? Where did more than 100,000 people settle in a single day? What state has the most American Indians? Where was baseball-great Mickey Mantle born? The answer to these questions is the Sooner State: Oklahoma!

*A picture map
of Oklahoma*

*Overleaf: Dog Run
Hollow, Wichita
Mountains National
Wildlife Refuge*

5

"Where the Wind Comes Sweepin' Down the Plain"

"Where the Wind Comes Sweepin' Down the Plain"

Oklahoma covers nearly 70,000 square miles of the United States Southwest. The Sooner State is easy to spot on a map. It looks like a hatchet. The handle sticks out from Oklahoma's northwestern corner. That land is called the Panhandle.

Only seventeen of the other forty-nine states are larger than Oklahoma.

Six states touch Oklahoma. Colorado and Kansas are to the north. Missouri and Arkansas are to the east. Texas is to the south and west. New Mexico is also to the west.

Oklahoma has many kinds of land. Much of it is flat land called plains. Mountains, hills, and plateaus cover the rest of Oklahoma. Mesas are another Oklahoma landform. These are steep, flat-topped mountains or hills. Black Mesa rises in the Panhandle. It is Oklahoma's highest point. Black Mesa stands 4,973 feet above sea level.

Swimmers at Turner Falls Park in the Arbuckle Mountains

Rivers, Lakes, Plants, and Animals

The Red River's color comes from clay and other materials in the water.

The Red River forms Oklahoma's wavy southern border. It flows 1,298 miles from New Mexico through Louisiana. The Arkansas River winds

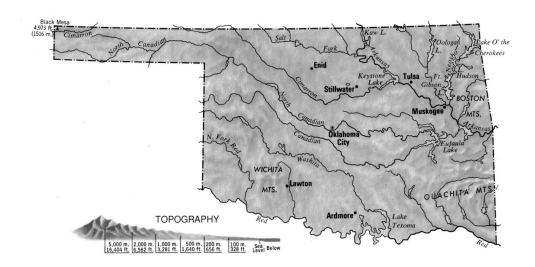

Black Mesa
4,973 ft.
(1516 m.)

TOPOGRAPHY

| 5,000 m. | 2,000 m. | 1,000 m. | 500 m. | 200 m. | 100 m. | Sea | Below |
| 16,404 ft. | 6,562 ft. | 3,281 ft. | 1,640 ft. | 656 ft. | 328 ft. | Level | |

through northeastern Oklahoma. Its total length is 1,460 miles. The Canadian, North Canadian, and Cimarron are other major rivers in Oklahoma. The state has about 100 small natural lakes. But it has twice as many artificially made lakes. Lake Eufaula covers about 160 square miles. It is the state's largest artificially made lake. Lake Texoma is another of those large lakes. It spills from Oklahoma into Texas.

About one-fifth of Oklahoma is forest. The redbud is the state tree. It is known for its red flowers. Oaks, walnuts, pines, elms, and mulberries grow in Oklahoma, too. Mistletoe is the state flower. It has

Water has collected in this granite boulder on Mount Scott in the Wichita Mountains.

9

Black-eyed Susans

Prairie dog

small yellow blossoms. Passionflowers also grow in Oklahoma. Some Sooners eat their fruit, called may-pops. Black-eyed Susans and violets are other Oklahoma wildflowers. Cactuses also grow in the state.

The buffalo is Oklahoma's state animal. Coyotes, prairie dogs, and armadillos live on the state's plains. Deer, foxes, and opossums make their homes in Oklahoma's forests. Cardinals, blue jays, ducks, wild turkeys, crows, and meadowlarks fly about. The scissor-tailed flycatcher is the state bird. It catches insects with its bill. Oklahoma's roadrunners stay on the ground. The white bass is the state fish. Catfish, sunfish, and carp also swim in Oklahoma's waters.

CLIMATE

Oklahoma's climate is generally warm and dry. Summers are hot there. Between May and September, temperatures sometimes reach 100 degrees Fahrenheit. Oklahomans need only a light jacket on most winter days. January temperatures often reach 50 degrees Fahrenheit.

Oklahomans suffer through many kinds of windstorms each year. After all, the state song says:

"Oklahoma, where the wind comes sweepin' down the plain." Rainstorms cause Oklahoma's rivers to flood. Yet the state is also subject to long dry spells. They are called droughts. Most of Oklahoma receives little snowfall. Now and then, giant wind-driven snowstorms do occur. They are called blizzards. More than fifty tornadoes rip through the Sooner State each year. These whirling wind-storms cause property damage and sometimes loss of life.

Left: Rock forms in Black Mesa State Park Right: Winter at Martin Park Nature Center, Oklahoma City

Overleaf: The Chisholm Trail, *by W. H. Jackson*

11

From Ancient Times Until Today

FROM ANCIENT TIMES UNTIL TODAY

Millions of years ago, dinosaurs lived in Oklahoma. The 90-foot diplodocus roamed about. It was the longest kind of dinosaur. The 80,000-pound apatosaurus lived there, too. Stegosaurus also tramped across the land. That dinosaur had bony plates on its back. Spikes stood up on its tail.

AMERICAN INDIANS

The first people reached Oklahoma about 20,000 years ago. The early Oklahomans lived in caves and along cliffs. Their drawings on cave walls have been found near Kenton. The ancient Oklahomans gathered berries. They also hunted elephant-like mammoths.

Between 1500 and 1800, several American Indian groups moved into Oklahoma. They included the Osage, Kiowa, Comanche, Arapaho, Wichita, and Caddo people. The Indians grew corn, beans, and squash. Many also hunted buffalo. They ate its meat. They made clothing and tepees from its skin. Tepees were cone-shaped tents. The Indians lived in

A Wichita grass house

14

them when they traveled. They built more permanent homes from wood and grass.

EUROPEAN EXPLORERS

Viking explorers from Greenland may have reached Oklahoma in 1012. At Poteau Mountain in Heavener, a huge stone bears that date. The lettering is in runic. This is an old kind of writing used by the Vikings. Some people think the Heavener Runestone is a fake. They don't believe that Vikings ever reached Oklahoma.

The Heavener Runestone

In 1541, Spanish explorers did arrive in Oklahoma. They hoped to find cities made of gold. Francisco Coronado came north from Mexico. He crossed Oklahoma's Panhandle. Hernando De Soto entered from the east. He traveled along the Arkansas River. Neither Coronado nor De Soto found any golden cities. But each claimed for Spain the lands they had crossed, including Oklahoma.

In 1682, La Salle explored the Mississippi River. He claimed all lands drained by the Mississippi for France. La Salle named the land Louisiana. That included present-day Oklahoma. In the early 1700s, a few French traders came to Oklahoma. They exchanged goods with the Indians for furs.

La Salle's full name was René-Robert Cavelier, Sieur de La Salle.

15

Neither France nor Spain had a strong hold on Oklahoma. In 1762, France gave all of Louisiana, including Oklahoma, to Spain. In 1800, Spain returned all of Louisiana to France. By then, only about 500 Europeans lived on Louisiana's Oklahoma land.

THE UNITED STATES EXPANDS WESTWARD

The United States of America was founded along the East Coast in 1776. By the 1800s, Americans wanted land to the west. In 1803, the United States bought Louisiana from France. Oklahoma was included.

A few Americans settled in Oklahoma in the early 1800s. Most were fur traders. In 1823, Auguste Pierre Chouteau established a trading post at present-day Salina. This was Oklahoma's first permanent non-Indian settlement.

In 1830, the United States Congress passed the Indian Removal Act. It allowed the government to move East Coast Indians to Oklahoma. Between 1830 and 1842, five southeastern tribes were pushed west. Those five tribes were the Seminoles, Creeks, Chickasaws, Choctaws, and Cherokees. They were called the Five Civilized Tribes by white

Between 1803 and statehood in 1907, Oklahoma was part of the following territories: Louisiana (1803-1812), Missouri (1812-1819), Arkansas (1819-1825), Indian (1825-1907), and Oklahoma (1890-1907).

16

people. Many of these Indians lived like the white people. They had towns with schools and churches. They grew crops and raised cattle. Some were rich and owned black slaves. White farmers and plantation owners wanted the Indians' rich lands.

This painting is one of artist Jerome Tiger's many depictions of the Trail of Tears.

THE TRAIL OF TEARS

Nearly 75,000 Indians made the long trip west. Thousands died of hunger, cold, and disease along the way. The Indians call their sad march to Oklahoma the "Trail of Tears."

The survivors settled in eastern and southern Oklahoma. This area was called Indian Territory. The United States government made a promise to those Indians. It said that the Oklahoma lands would be theirs forever. Each tribe had its own land. The tribes were like separate countries. Each had its own capital, government, and leaders. The Indians built farms and towns in their new homeland. They raised corn, cotton, and cattle.

This 1875 photo shows the Creek Council House at Okmulgee.

The Civil War

The northern and southern states had different views on many subjects. One of them was slavery. In 1861, the Civil War began. Eleven slave-holding southern states formed the Confederacy. They fought the northern states, or the Union. Oklahoma's Five Civilized Tribes owned slaves. They also disliked the United States government for moving them west. About 6,000 men from Indian Territory fought for the South. Stand Watie, a Cherokee, led the Cherokee Mounted Rifles. Other Indians joined and fought with the Union.

The North won the war in 1865. The northern victory freed the country's remaining slaves. Many of the Oklahoma Indians' former slaves were adopted by the tribes that had owned them.

In 1866, the United States government took land from the Five Civilized Tribes. This was to punish them for helping the South. Tribes from farther west were then moved into Indian Territory.

Cowboys, Boomers, and Sooners

Growing numbers of white people also entered Oklahoma. Cowboys drove long-horned cattle from

General Stand Watie (above) was said to have been the last Confederate general to surrender.

19

An early cattle roundup in western Oklahoma

Texas to Kansas. They followed the Shawnee and the Chisholm trails through Oklahoma. Between 1870 and 1872, the Missouri-Kansas-Texas Railroad was built through eastern Oklahoma. Soon trains brought thousands of white people to Oklahoma.

A number of white farmers rented land from the Indians. Many whites worked in coal mines on Indian land. Others taught in Indian schools. In the 1880s, "Boomers" from Kansas led thousands of pioneers into Indian Territory. The Boomers wanted some Indian land opened for white settlement. Time after time, United States troops forced the pioneers back to Kansas.

In 1889, the Boomers got what they wanted. The United States government bought about 5,000 square miles of Indian land. It was in the middle of Oklahoma. The land was opened to settlers at noon on April 22, 1889. Each family could claim 160 acres. Soldiers tried to keep people from entering the land too early. But some sneaked in "sooner" than they were supposed to. They were called Sooners. That nickname spread to all Oklahomans.

At noon on April 22, bugles sounded and guns were fired. The Land Run of 1889 began. Thousands raced off to make their claims. They rode on horseback and in wagons. Some went on

trains, jumping off when they spotted land they liked. People even pedaled along on bicycles. Others ran on foot.

About 50,000 settlers arrived on that day. By day's end, Guthrie was a tent city of 15,000 people. Oklahoma City, Kingfisher, Stillwater, and Norman were also begun on that day. Some settlers soon built log houses. Others cut up chunks of sod. They made sod houses.

In 1890, the United States Congress formed the Oklahoma Territory. It was west of Indian Territory. Oklahoma then had two parts. Indian Territory had 180,000 people. Oklahoma Territory had 78,000 people. Together, they were called the "Twin Territories."

These men were holding down a town lot in Guthrie during the Land Run of 1889. Guthrie became known as the "Magic City" because it began so quickly.

Huge crowds of people gathered for the Cherokee Outlet land run in 1893. The Cherokee Outlet was also called the Cherokee Strip.

Sequoyah, a Cherokee leader, came to Oklahoma in the 1830s. He invented the Cherokee alphabet.

During the 1890s, the United States government bought more Indian lands. More land runs were held. The biggest of them took place in northern Oklahoma. On September 16, 1893, more than 100,000 people rushed into the Cherokee Outlet.

By the 1900s, the Twin Territories had enough people for statehood. The big question was: Should there be two states or one? The Indians wanted their own state. It would be called Sequoyah. Instead, the Twin Territories became the state of Oklahoma. On November 16, 1907, Oklahoma entered the Union as the forty-sixth state. Guthrie was the Sooner State's first capital. In 1910, Oklahoma City became the permanent capital.

OIL, WORLD WARS, AND DEPRESSION

In 1901, oil was found near Tulsa. Many oil companies set up business in Tulsa. The city became known as the "Oil Capital of the World." In 1917, Frank Phillips founded the Phillips Petroleum Company in Bartlesville. Ardmore, Ponca City, and Oklahoma City also became oil boomtowns.

Natural-gas deposits were found near the oil deposits.

Also in 1917, the United States entered World War I (1914-1918). Oklahoma sent about 90,000 troops to war. Company E of the 142nd Infantry

A view of Main Street, Oklahoma City, in the mid-1890s

was an Oklahoma fighting group. It was made up mostly of Indians. Oklahoma oil, cotton, and food crops helped win the war.

The Great Depression (1929-1939) brought hard times to the United States. The Sooner State was especially hard hit. Oklahoma and many other states suffered several years of drought. Western Oklahoma was part of the Dust Bowl. After winds blew across the land, dust covered homes and towns. The dust and dry weather killed crops and livestock. Factory workers lost their jobs. Banks closed. About 60,000 Sooners left the state. Most headed for California. There, they were called Okies.

During the depression and dust-bowl years, thousands of Oklahoma families packed up their belongings and headed out of the state to look for work.

World War II (1939-1945) helped end the depression. Improved weather helped, too. Oklahomans built airplanes and weapons. The state's miners and farmers sent supplies to the troops. More than 200,000 Sooners in uniform helped win the war.

A repair hangar at Tinker Air Force Base during World War II

RECENT GROWTH AND CHANGE

Between 1947 and 1970, the McClellan-Kerr Arkansas River Navigation System was built. Through it, the Arkansas River's channels were deepened and widened. Dams and locks were also built on the river. Large vessels can now travel

John McClellan was a senator from Arkansas and Robert Kerr was a senator from Oklahoma. They backed the river project in the Senate.

25

through Oklahoma on the Arkansas River. Tulsa and Muskogee have become important ports. So has the small town of Catoosa. These ports have helped Oklahoma's businesses.

Dams were also built on other Oklahoma rivers. They help prevent floods. The dams also turn water power into electricity. Lakes were formed behind the dams. They are used for fishing, boating, and swimming. Tenkiller, Oologah, and Eufaula are a few of those lakes.

Manufacturing grew in Oklahoma in the 1960s and 1970s. Airplane and rocket companies moved there. So did firms that make automobile parts and computers. Growth continued because of high oil prices. Thousands of newcomers settled in Oklahoma. They came to work for Oklahoma's oil and gas companies. The state's population rose by 466,000 during the 1970s.

The 1970s were also good for many Oklahoma Indians. The Cherokees, Chickasaws, and Choctaws regained 96 miles of the Arkansas River. The riverbed has oil, gas, and gravel deposits. Money from mining the riverbed is used to better those Indians' lives.

In the 1980s, Oklahoma again suffered hard times. Cheap oil flowed into the country. Oil prices

An Oklahoma oil refinery

Natural gas is used to heat homes and to run ovens. Oil is refined for fuels used to run cars and airplanes.

fell. This hurt Oklahoma badly. Many miners and factory workers lost their jobs. Banks failed across the state. Farm earnings dropped, too. About 18,000 farmers lost their land.

The lives of many Oklahomans improved in the 1990s. In 1993, the state began its Quality Jobs Program. Companies that hire Oklahomans get money from the state. This program has created thousands of full-time jobs. Oklahoma's leaders hope that most Sooners will have jobs by the year 2000.

People use the ledge of a dam to fish in Lake Rush.

Overleaf: A child in a headdress at the Red Earth Indian Festival

27

Oklahomans and Their Work

OKLAHOMANS AND THEIR WORK

The 1990 census counted more than 3.1 million Oklahomans. Four out of five Oklahomans are white. Many of them have German, Irish, Polish, or Russian backgrounds. Nearly 250,000 Oklahomans are black. Hispanics number nearly 100,000. Most of these people have family roots in Mexico. The number of Asian Oklahomans doubled to 35,000 between 1980 and 1990. Many of the state's Asian people are from Vietnam.

More than 250,000 Oklahomans are American Indians. No other state has as many. The Cherokees make up the state's largest Indian group. There are 80,000 Cherokees in Oklahoma. About sixty other Indian groups also live in the Sooner State. Among them are the Chickasaws, Choctaws, Creeks, Seminoles, and Osages.

THEIR WORK

About half of all Oklahomans have jobs. Sales, service, and government workers hold most jobs in Oklahoma. Each of these fields hires about 275,000

Veterans' Day ceremonies, Oklahoma City

A Czech festival in Yukon

workers. Tinker Air Force Base alone has 22,000 workers. This base is the state's largest employer.

About 165,000 Oklahomans make products. Automobiles, airplanes, and their parts are the top manufactured goods. Rocket parts, oil-field machinery, and tires are other leading goods. Only Alabamians make more tires. Refined oil and telephone parts are other Oklahoma products. Many Sooner-packaged meats and baked goods start on Oklahoma farms.

Oklahoma has about 73,000 farmers and ranchers. They are the fourth-largest raisers of beef cattle

Left: Checking out the animals at the Oklahoma State Fair Right: A roadside watermelon vendor, Ponca City

in the country. Oklahoma ranchers have 5.5 million cattle. Only two states raise more horses than Oklahoma. Wheat is the state's leading farm crop. Only Kansas and North Dakota grow more. The state also has large harvests of hay and sorghum. Those crops are used as animal feed. Oklahoma is also among the top growers of pecans, peanuts, watermelons, and cotton.

Oklahoma has about 35,000 miners. Only Texas and Louisiana have more. Oklahomans produce the third-largest amount of natural gas in the country. Sooners also mine the fifth-largest amount of oil. Oklahoma has the country's only iodine mines. Iodine is used to clean germs from cuts and scrapes.

A family canoeing in Little River State Park

Overleaf: The Oklahoma State Capitol, in Oklahoma City

31

A Trip Through the Sooner State

A Trip Through the Sooner State

Oklahomans and visitors alike enjoy the Sooner State's cities, prairies, and woods, its rivers, canyons, and hills. Oklahoma's many fascinating museums explain the state's Indian, pioneer, and mining history.

The Panhandle

The Panhandle's three counties have only 26,000 people. Cimarron County doesn't have even a single stoplight! The Panhandle is best known for its sorghum and helium.

Black Mesa State Park is in the Panhandle's northwestern tip. Black Mesa, the state's highest point, stands there. The park has picture writings carved in rocks. They were made by ancient people 1,500 years ago. Petrified wood is found there, too. Over many years, minerals in water turned the wood to stone. Many dinosaur bones have also been uncovered in the park.

To the southeast is Boise City. The remains of Fort Nichols lie near there today. In 1865, frontier scout Kit Carson began the fort. It was built to pro-

Lake Carl Etling, in Black Mesa State Park

tect wagon trains on the Santa Fe Trail. This famous trail linked Missouri with New Mexico.

Guymon is east of Boise City. This town sits on one of the world's largest natural-gas deposits. Optima National Wildlife Refuge is nearby. Bird-watchers can sight sandhill cranes and least terns there.

Beaver is near the Panhandle's eastern end. The Jones and Plummer Trail Museum is there. One display includes a stove that burned cow chips. There are few trees on the Panhandle, so pioneers gathered cow dung. They let it dry, and then burned it. Now, each spring, Beaver hosts the World Cow Chip Throwing Contest. The man and woman who throw chips the farthest win prizes.

Selecting cow chips for the World Cow Chip Throwing Contest held each spring in Beaver

OTHER NORTHERN OKLAHOMA HIGHLIGHTS

Just east of the Panhandle is Woodward. It is home to the Plains Indians and Pioneers Museum. Visitors can see Indian beadwork and warbonnets there. A sheriff's office and jail cell form part of the museum.

To the northeast is Alabaster Caverns. It is the world's largest gypsum cave. Underground water has fashioned interesting rooms and shapes in the rock. Gun Barrel Tunnel and the Bathtubs look like their names.

Alabaster Caverns are also called Bat Caves because millions of bats live there.

A pioneer bedroom at the Museum of the Cherokee Strip in Enid

Enid is to the east. It was founded during the 1893 Land Rush. Displays at Enid's Cherokee Strip Museum tell about that exciting time. The Railroad Museum of Oklahoma is also in Enid. There, visitors learn how railroads helped Oklahoma and the country grow. They helped make Enid a flour-milling center. Oklahoma's largest flour mill is in the town.

Ponca City is about an hour's drive northeast of Enid. The Pioneer Woman Statue and Museum are there. The statue honors the women who settled the frontier. The museum shows what frontier home life was like.

Pawhuska is due east of Ponca City. Osage Indian headquarters are there. Visitors to Pawhuska can learn much at the Osage Tribal Museum. Osage beadwork, feather work, and costumes are displayed.

To the northeast is Bartlesville. Oklahoma's first major oil well still stands there. The Nellie Johnstone Oil Well dates from 1897. The Prairie National Wild Horse Refuge is nearby. About 1,500 wild mustangs run free there. The Woolaroc Museum is also near Bartlesville. Navajo Indian blankets are among its treasures. The museum is on the grounds of oilman Frank Phillips' ranch. Today, buffalo, elk, and long-horned cattle roam the land.

The Pioneer Woman Statue in Ponca City

To the south is Tulsa. This town got started in 1879 as a mail stop. The town's population soared after the big 1901 oil strike. Tulsa today has about 367,000 people. It is the second-biggest city in the Sooner State.

Tulsa is known for its art museums. The Gilcrease Museum displays Thomas Gilcrease's art collection. He was a wealthy oilman of Creek descent. Western art by Frederic Remington and Charles Russell are among its highlights. The Philbrook Museum of Art was the home of another wealthy oilman. Indian paintings, baskets, and pottery now grace the Waite Phillips' home. African sculptures and paintings about the oil industry can also be seen there. The Fenster Museum of Jewish Art is also in Tulsa. There, visitors can see a 4,000-year-old menorah.

The Oklahoma Jazz Hall of Fame is in Tulsa. Charles Christian and Chet Baker, two Oklahomans, are honored there. The Oxley Nature Center is another Tulsa landmark. The center is in Mohawk Park. That is the city's largest park. Armadillos live there. The nature center also has red-eared pond sliders. They are a kind of turtle.

CENTRAL OKLAHOMA

Tahlequah is in east-central Oklahoma. It is the Cherokee people's capital. Visitors to the Cherokee Heritage Center learn much about Oklahoma's biggest tribe. A Cherokee village from the 1600s has been rebuilt there. Each summer, the center offers *The Trail of Tears*. This play tells the Cherokees' story from the 1830s to statehood.

Muskogee is southeast of Tahlequah. It has the Five Civilized Tribes Museum. There, visitors can learn about the Cherokees, Chickasaws, Choctaws, Creeks, and Seminoles. Fort Gibson is near

This painting of Pueblo Indians by Martin Hennings can be seen at the Gilcrease Museum.

Children at the Cherokee Heritage Center in Tahlequah

39

The Buffalo Bill Cody statue at the National Cowboy Hall of Fame

Paintings at the National Cowboy Hall of Fame

Muskogee. It dates from 1824. Both Robert E. Lee and Jefferson Davis served there. Later, both became famous southern Civil War leaders.

To the west is Oklahoma City. It is in the middle of the Sooner State. Oklahoma City has about 445,000 people. That makes it Oklahoma's largest city. Since 1910, Oklahoma City has also been the state capital. Oklahoma lawmakers meet in the state capitol. For years, oil was pumped from under the building. Oil rigs still stand outside the state capitol today.

Oklahoma City honors its cowboy and pioneer history. The National Cowboy Hall of Fame and

The Red Earth Festival Parade

Western Heritage Center is there. A pioneer town and sod house have been rebuilt within the building. The Rodeo Hall of Fame is there, too. It honors Oklahoma's rodeo stars. They include six-time national champion Tom Ferguson and four-time champ Jim Shoulders.

Each fall, Oklahoma City hosts one of the country's best state fairs. About 2 million people attend. The festivities include a rodeo and American Indian dancing. Oklahoma City also honors the state's Indian history. Each June, Oklahoma City hosts the Red Earth Native American Cultural Festival. This is

North America's largest gathering of Indians. More than 1,200 Indian dancers gather there. They come from around the United States and Canada. The festival also offers Indian art and food.

Guthrie is north of Oklahoma City. It was Oklahoma's territorial capital. Guthrie's Oklahoma Territorial Museum tells about life in those early years. The town celebrates the great Land Run of 1889 every year during Eighty-Niner Week. That land run marked the beginning of Guthrie.

Norman is a few miles south of Oklahoma City. Norman's 80,000 people place it fourth among Oklahoma's cities. Norman is also home to the University of Oklahoma. This giant school has about 20,000 students. The University of Oklahoma Sooners have won six national football titles.

Southwest of Norman is Anadarko. It is known for Indian City U.S.A. Villages of seven Indian groups have been rebuilt there. They show how Pueblo, Caddo, Kiowa, Wichita, Apache, Navajo, and Pawnee people lived. The National Hall of Fame for Famous American Indians is also in Anadarko. Apache warrior Geronimo is honored there. So is Cheyenne chief Black Kettle. Black Kettle wanted to live in peace with white people.

A Pawnee earth lodge at Indian City U.S.A.

Near Oklahoma's western border is the town of Cheyenne. West of town is Washita Battlefield. There, in 1868, troops under General George Custer attacked sleeping Cheyennes. About 100 of them were killed. Black Kettle and his wife were among the dead. The Black Kettle Museum is close to the battlefield. It is a good place to learn about the Cheyenne people.

SOUTHERN OKLAHOMA

Altus is near Oklahoma's southwest corner. The Museum of the Western Prairie is there. It displays mammoth and mastodon bones. Children also

The Eighty-Niner Week parade in Guthrie

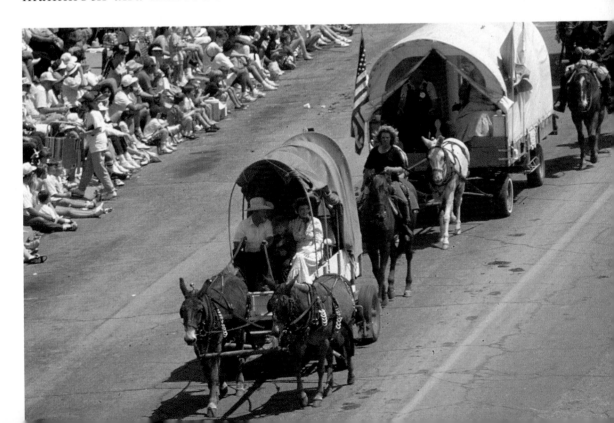

The chuck-wagon exhibit at the Museum of the Western Prairie

enjoy the museum's chuck wagon. Cowboys were served food from chuck wagons during the long cattle drives.

Fort Sill is east of Altus. The fort was begun in 1869. Geronimo was imprisoned there. He is buried in the fort's Apache cemetery. Today, soldiers learn to shoot cannons and rockets at Fort Sill. Close by is the Wichita Mountains Wildlife Refuge. More than 600 buffalo live there. At one time, millions of buffalo roamed America's plains. By the late 1800s, they had almost disappeared. White hunters had killed most of them. Now, they are raised where they can be protected.

To the east is Lawton. This is Oklahoma's third-largest city. Lawton is home to the Museum of the Great Plains. It has displays about Indians, fur traders, and cowboys. Visitors enjoy the rebuilt fur-trading post.

To the southeast is Ardmore. Its public library houses the Eliza Cruce Hall Doll Museum. Eliza collected 300 dolls from around the world. Some are made of wax, wood, or leather. Others are made of china.

Farther southeast is Durant. Nearby are the ruins of Fort Washita. The fort was built in 1842. Soldiers were there to protect the Chickasaws and

Choctaws. During the Civil War, southern soldiers kept supplies there.

Hugo is due east of Durant. The Hugo Heritage Railroad takes visitors on 45-mile journeys. The riders travel through woods and over rivers. One route goes over the Red River into Texas. Riders may spot deer and wild turkeys.

Idabel is near the Red River in southeast Oklahoma. It is a good place to end an Oklahoma tour. The town was built on a Choctaw Indian's land. It was named for his daughters, Ida and Belle. Idabel houses the Museum of the Red River. Its displays tell about life among the Choctaw and Caddo Indians.

The Hugo Heritage Train

An inside view of the Hugo Heritage Train

A GALLERY OF FAMOUS SOONERS

Many Sooners have achieved fame. They include baseball stars, dancers, and children's authors.

Alice Mary Robertson (1854-1931) was born near Muskogee. There, in 1884, she founded a school for Creek students. Robertson was also Muskogee's postmistress. And she founded its Red Cross office. In 1920, "Miss Alice" was elected to the U.S. Congress. She became the second woman to serve in the House of Representatives (1921-1923).

Carl Albert was born in Bugtussle in 1908. He also became a famous lawmaker. Albert served Oklahoma in the U. S. House of Representatives for thirty years (1947-1977). He was Speaker of the House from 1971 to 1977.

Many "Wild West" shows were once based in Oklahoma. These traveling shows featured trick riding, shooting, and roping. The 101 Ranch near Ponca City had a famous Wild West show. **Bill Pickett** (1871?-1932) was one of its stars. He was a black cowboy. Pickett invented "bulldogging." In that event, a cowboy wrestles a wild steer to the

Opposite: Will Rogers with his daughter Mary

In 1917, Jeannette Rankin of Montana became the first woman in Congress.

Carl Albert

Each state is allowed
to have statues of two
famous people in the
U.S. Capitol in
Washington, D.C.
Oklahoma's are of
Sequoyah and Will
Rogers.

Woody Guthrie

ground. **Lucille Mulhall** (1875?-1940) was raised near Guthrie. She starred in her father's Wild West show. Mulhall also entered rodeos. She was known as the "World's First Cowgirl."

Will Rogers (1879-1935) was born near Oologah. He grew up on a cattle ranch. There he learned to ride horses and rope cattle. Rogers became an entertainer. He did rope tricks while he talked about politics and people. Rogers starred in plays and movies. He also wrote a newspaper column.

Oral Roberts was born near Ada in 1918. He is part Cherokee. Roberts became a popular preacher on radio and television. He founded Tulsa's Oral Roberts University in 1963.

Woody Guthrie (1912-1967) was born in Okemah. At the age of fifteen, he left home with his harmonica. Guthrie traveled the country, singing for his meals. He became a great writer and singer of folk songs. Many of them were about poor farmers and factory workers. "This Land Is Your Land" is his most famous song.

Today, two country music superstars are Oklahomans. **Reba McEntire** was born in McAlester in 1955. She has sold over 20 million albums since then. **Garth Brooks** was born in Tulsa in 1962. He writes songs and sings them. "The Thunder Rolls" and "If Tomorrow Never Comes" are two of his songs.

Five Oklahomans became famous ballerinas. All of them claim a Native American heritage. **Maria Tallchief** (born 1925) was the daughter of an Osage chief. Tallchief was the first American-trained ballerina to become a world star. She founded the Chicago City Ballet. Her sister **Marjorie Tallchief** (born 1927) danced with the Paris Ballet Company. **Yvonne Chouteau** (born 1929) danced with the Ballet Russe de Monte Carlo at age fourteen. She was the youngest American ever to join that group. Chouteau later taught dance at the University of Oklahoma. **Moscelyne Larkin** (born 1925) was co-director of the Tulsa Civic Ballet. **Rozella Hightower** (born 1920) opened a ballet school in Cannes, France.

Several Oklahomans became fine authors. **Angie Debo** (1890-1988) was born in Kansas. As a child, she came to Marshall, Oklahoma, in a covered wagon. Later, Debo taught history in an Enid high school. She was an expert on Indian history. Her books include *Geronimo: The Man, His Time, His Place.*

Claremore-born **Lynn Riggs** (1899-1954) became a playwright. His best-known play is *Green*

Maria Tallchief

Grow the Lilacs. The Broadway show *Oklahoma!* was based on it. **Harold Keith** was born in Lambert in 1903. He became a children's author. Keith's *Rifles for Watie* won the 1958 Newbery Medal. The book was based on General Stand Watie's experiences. **Ralph Ellison** (1914-1994) was born in Oklahoma City. He wrote about what it was like to be black in America. Ellison's novel *Invisible Man* won the 1953 National Book Award.

Susan Eloise (S. E.) Hinton was born in Tulsa in 1950. At the age of fifteen, she began writing *The Outsiders.* This novel is about troubled teens and gangs. Later, Hinton also wrote *That Was Then, This Is Now; Rumble Fish;* and *Tex.* All of these young people's books were made into movies.

Chester Gould (1900-1985) was born in Pawnee. At the age of twelve, he won five dollars in a cartooning contest. Gould later created the cartoon strip "Dick Tracy." Millions of readers have followed the adventures of the square-jawed crime fighter. **Jerome Tiger** (1914-1967) was born in Tahlequah. He was part Creek and part Seminole. Tiger painted scenes of Indian life and stories. He created hundreds of beautiful works in his short life.

Many Sooners have become actors. Movie actor **Van Heflin** (1910-1971) was a Walters native. In

Chester Gould

1942, he won an Academy Award for *Johnny Eager.* He also appeared in *Shane,* a famous Western. **Tony Randall** was born in Tulsa in 1920. He starred in "The Odd Couple" on television. **James Garner** was born in Norman in 1928. He is part Cherokee. Garner starred on television in "Maverick." He was also in *Maverick,* the 1994 movie. **Alfre Woodard** was born in Tulsa in 1953. She appeared in "Hill Street Blues" and "St. Elsewhere" on television. Woodard also starred in the 1994 movie *Crooklyn.* **Ron Howard** was born in Duncan in 1954. He became a television star when he was only six. Howard played Opie on "The Andy Griffith Show." Later, he played Richie on "Happy Days." When Howard grew up, he became a movie director. Howard's films include *Splash* and *Cocoon.*

Many Oklahomans became sports stars. **Jim Thorpe** (1887-1953) was born near Prague. He was the great-grandson of Sauk chief Black Hawk. Thorpe won two gold medals at the 1912 Olympics in Sweden. They were for events in track and field. The king of Sweden called Thorpe the "World's Greatest Athlete." Later, Thorpe starred in major league baseball and pro football.

Mickey Mantle (1931-1995) was born in Spavinaw. This Yankee star won four home-run

Jim Thorpe

Mickey Mantle

*Leroy Gordon
Cooper, Jr.*

Thomas Stafford

crowns. His homers include a 565-foot blast. That is one of the farthest in history. **Willie Stargell** was born in Earlsboro in 1941. He won two home-run crowns. Catcher **Johnny Bench** also won two home-run titles. Bench was born in Oklahoma City in 1947. He helped the Cincinnati Reds win two World Series championships (1975 and 1976). Mantle, Stargell, and Bench are all in the Baseball Hall of Fame.

Three Oklahomans became famous astronauts. **Leroy Gordon Cooper, Jr.,** was born in Shawnee in 1927. At age sixteen, he flew a plane by himself. In 1959, he became one of America's first astronauts. During the 1960s, he made two separate flights around the earth. **Thomas Stafford** was born in Weatherford in 1930. In 1969, he commanded the *Apollo 10* flight. It came within 9 miles of the moon. **William Pogue** was born in Okemah in 1930. He spent eighty-four days aboard *Skylab 4.* That was the longest space flight up to that time.

Wilma Mankiller was born in Tahlequah in 1945. She is half Cherokee. Mankiller works to improve housing, jobs, and education for her people. In 1985, she became the Cherokee's main chief. She was the first woman of any tribe to hold that office.

The birthplace of Wilma Mankiller, Will Rogers, Woody Guthrie, and Maria Tallchief . . .

Home also to Angie Debo, Geronimo, and Bill Pickett . . .

A place where more than 100,000 people arrived in a single day . . .

Today, a leading producer of wheat, horses, oil, and natural gas . . .

This is the Sooner State—Oklahoma!

Johnny Bench is on the right in this Hall of Fame induction picture.

53

Did You Know?

The town of Texhoma is partly in Oklahoma and partly in Texas.

Gordon Graham of Edmond set a record for growing the world's biggest tomato in 1986. It weighed nearly eight pounds. The year before, he grew the world's tallest tomato plant. It was 53.5 feet tall.

From 1875 to 1907, Bass Reeves, a former slave, served as a U.S. deputy marshal in the Oklahoma Territory. He sent many outlaws to federal prison.

Oklahoma has more sites relating to American Indians than any other state. Many Oklahoma tribes consider themselves separate nations within the United States. They have their own capitals, chiefs, and museums.

The town of Okay, in northeastern Oklahoma, was once called Sleepyville.

Elias Boudinot, a Cherokee Indian, helped found Vinita. He named the town for Vinnie Ream, a female sculptor whom he loved.

The Sooners from the University of Oklahoma won the 1994 College World Series of baseball.

Oklahomans invented both the shopping cart and the turn signal for the automobile.

Seventeen Oklahoma towns have the same names as United States presidents: Washington, Adams, Jefferson, Monroe, Taylor, Fillmore, Pierce, Lincoln, Johnson, Grant, Cleveland, Roosevelt, Taft, Wilson, Carter, Reagan, and Clinton.

Once in Ponca City, while a husband and wife were eating supper, a tornado lifted their house off the ground. Most of the house was blown to bits. But the floor was set back down on the ground with the couple safely on it.

Nearly one-half of Oklahoma's households have dogs. That is the highest percentage in the country.

Patience Latting was elected mayor of Oklahoma City in 1971. She was one of the first woman mayors in the United States for a city with over 200,000 people.

The country's first parking meter was installed at Oklahoma City in 1935.

Other Oklahoma towns with unusual names include Bowlegs, Frogville, and Jumbo.

Maude Thomas came to Beaver in a covered wagon in 1886 when she was five. By the age of twenty-one, she had bought the *Beaver Herald*. Thomas was Oklahoma's first woman newspaper publisher.

Oklahoma Information

State flag

Scissor-tailed flycatcher

Redbud blossoms

Area: 69,956 square miles (the eighteenth-biggest state)

Greatest Distance North to South: 231 miles

Greatest Distance East to West: 478 miles

Borders: Colorado and Kansas to the north; Missouri and Arkansas to the east; Texas to the south and west; New Mexico to the west

Highest Point: Black Mesa, 4,973 feet above sea level

Lowest Point: Along the Little River in the southeast corner, 287 feet above sea level

Hottest Recorded Temperature: 120° F. (six times; most recently at Tipton, on June 27, 1994)

Coldest Recorded Temperature: -27° F. (at Vinita, on February 13, 1905, and at Watts, on January 18, 1930)

Statehood: The forty-sixth state, on November 16, 1907

Origin of Name: In the 1860s, Allen Wright, a Choctaw Indian, coined the name *Oklahoma;* it means "red people" in the Choctaw language

Capital: Oklahoma City (since 1910)

Counties: 77

United States Representatives: 6

State Senators: 48

State Representatives: 101

State Song: "Oklahoma!" by Oscar Hammerstein II (words) and Richard Rodgers (music)

State Motto: *Labor Omnia Vincit* (Latin, meaning "Labor Conquers All Things")

Nicknames: "Sooner State," "Boomer State"

State Seal: Adopted in 1907

State Flag: Adopted in 1925

State Wildflower: Indian blanket
State Bird: Scissor-tailed flycatcher
State Folk Dance: Square dance
State Musical Instrument: Fiddle
State Animal: American buffalo (bison)
State Game Animal: White-tailed deer
State Furbearing Animal: Raccoon
State Reptile: Mountain boomer lizard

State Flower: Mistletoe
State Tree: Redbud
State Fish: White bass
State Insect: Honeybee
State Colors: Green and white

American buffalo (bison) and calf

Some Rivers: Red, Arkansas, Canadian, North Canadian, Cimarron, Verdigris, Neosho, Washita

Some Mountain Ranges: Wichita, Arbuckle, and Ouachita

Wildlife: Deer, foxes, raccoons, coyotes, prairie dogs, armadillos, buffalo, bobcats, rattlesnakes, copperhead snakes, lizards, cardinals, blue jays, ducks, wild turkeys, geese, pheasants, sandhill cranes, sandpipers, roadrunners, many other kinds of birds, white bass, catfish, sunfish, carp, many other kinds of fish

Manufactured Products: Airplane parts, rocket parts, cars, other transportation equipment, oil-field equipment and other machinery, tires, refined oil, meat and other foods, telephone parts, glass and clay goods

Farm Products: Beef cattle, horses, chickens, hogs, sheep, wheat, hay, corn, sorghum, soybeans, pecans, peanuts, peaches, watermelons, cotton

Mining Products: Natural gas, oil, iodine, coal, crushed stone, sand and gravel

Population: 3,145,585, twenty-eighth among the fifty states (1990 U.S. Census Bureau figures)

Major Cities (1990 Census):

White-tailed deer

Mountain boomer lizard

Oklahoma City	444,719	Edmond	52,315
Tulsa	367,302	Midwest City	52,267
Lawton	80,561	Enid	45,309
Norman	80,071	Moore	40,318
Broken Arrow	58,043	Muskogee	37,708

Oklahoma History

18,000 B.C.—The first people reach Oklahoma

A.D. 1012—Vikings possibly reach Oklahoma

1541—Spanish explorers Francisco Coronado and Hernando De Soto reach Oklahoma in separate expeditions

1682—La Salle claims a huge area, including Oklahoma, for France and names it Louisiana

1762—France gives Louisiana, including Oklahoma, to Spain

1800—Spain returns Louisiana, including Oklahoma, to France

1803—France sells Louisiana, including Oklahoma, to the United States

1823—At present-day Salina, Auguste Pierre Chouteau establishes a trading post that is Oklahoma's first permanent non-Indian settlement

1830—The Indian Removal Act is passed

1830-42—The Five Civilized Tribes are forcibly moved to Oklahoma

1834—The U.S. government creates the Indian Territory

1844—Oklahoma's first newspaper, the *Cherokee Advocate*, is published by Cherokees at Tahlequah

1861-65—About 6,000 Oklahoma Indians help the South during the Civil War

1865—The North's victory frees the country's remaining slaves, including those owned by Oklahoma Indians

1866—The U.S. government punishes Oklahoma Indians for helping the South by taking away some land and distributing it to other tribes

1880s—Boomers want Oklahoma opened to white settlement

1889—The United States buys land from the Creeks and Seminoles and opens much of it to settlers

1890—The Oklahoma Territory is created; it and Indian Territory are called the "Twin Territories"

A Civil War reenactment of the Battle of Middle Boggy

1890s—The U.S. government buys more Indian lands

1892—The University of Oklahoma opens at Norman

1893—On September 16, in the biggest Oklahoma land run, more than 100,000 people rush into the Cherokee Outlet

1901—Oil is found in the Tulsa area

1905—The Indians try unsuccessfully to create their own state of Sequoyah

1907—On November 16, the Twin Territories become Oklahoma, the forty-sixth state

1910—Oklahoma City becomes the permanent state capital

1917-18—Oklahoma sends about 90,000 troops to help win World War I

1929-39—The Great Depression causes widespread joblessness in Oklahoma and other states

1941-45—Oklahoma sends more than 200,000 men and women to help win World War II

1953—The Turner Turnpike from Oklahoma City to Tulsa is completed

1970—The McClellan-Kerr Arkansas River Navigation System opens

1971—Patience Latting takes office as Oklahoma City's mayor, becoming one of the first woman mayors of a U.S. city of over 200,000 people

1974—At age thirty-three, David Boren is elected Oklahoma's governor, becoming one of the youngest people ever elected a state governor

1980—Oklahoma is part of a big area hit by drought

1986—Heavy rains cause over $140 million in flood damage

1990—The Sooner State's population reaches 3,145,585

1995—On April 19, a bomb explodes at the Alfred Murrah Federal Building in Oklahoma City, killing 168 people

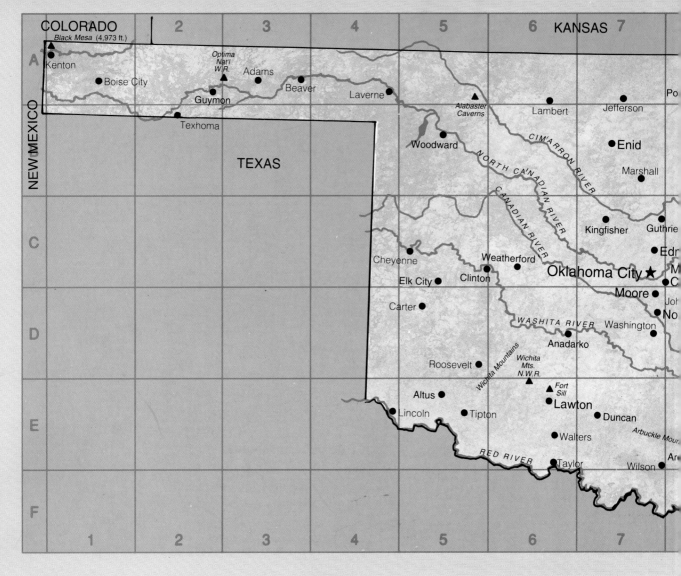

MAP KEY

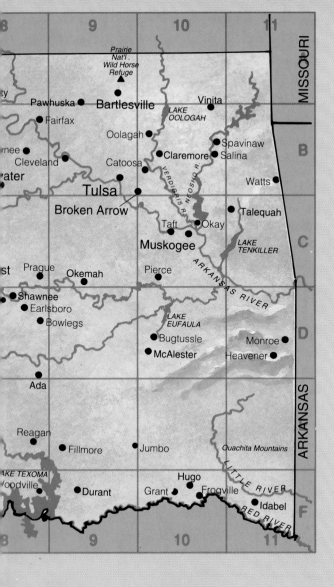

GLOSSARY

artificial: Made by people rather than occurring naturally

astronaut: A person who is highly trained for spaceflight

blizzard: A snowstorm driven by very high winds

capital: The city that is the seat of government

capitol: The building in which the government meets

climate: The typical weather of a region

drought: A period when rainfall is far below normal

explorer: A person who visits and studies unknown lands

mammoths and mastodons: Prehistoric animals that were much like elephants

manufacturing: The making of products

mesa: A flat-topped mountain or hill

million: A thousand thousand (1,000,000)

panhandle: A piece of land shaped like the handle of a pan

permanent: Lasting

pioneer: A person who is among the first to move into a region

plains: Rather flat lands

population: The number of people in a place

rodeo: An event at which cowboys and cowgirls compete at riding and roping

territory: Land owned by a country

tornado: A powerful windstorm that comes from a whirling, funnel-shaped cloud

PICTURE ACKNOWLEDGMENTS

Front cover, ©Steve Vidler/**SuperStock**; 1, ©**Tom Dietrich**; 2, Tom Dunnington; 3, Courtesy Mike Larsen; 4-5, Tom Dunnington; 6-7, ©**James P. Rowan**; 8, ©**Tom Dietrich**; 9 (top), Courtesy of Hammond Incorporated, Maplewood, New Jersey; 9 (bottom), ©**Tom Dietrich**; 10 (top), Pat Wadecki/**Root Resources**; 10 (bottom), Rod Planck/**Dembinsky Photo Assoc.**; 11 (left), ©**Tom Till**; 11 (right), Oklahoma Tourism Photo by Fred W. Marvel; 12-13, Scotts Bluff National Monument; 14, Steve Vidler/**SuperStock**; 15, ©**Tom Till**; 17, Courtesy Peggy Tiger; 18, Archives and Manuscripts Division of the Oklahoma Historical Society; 19, Archives and Manuscripts Division of the Oklahoma Historical Society; 20, Archives and Manuscripts Division of the Oklahoma Historical Society; 21, Archives and Manuscripts Division of the Oklahoma Historical Society; 22, Archives and Manuscripts Division of the Oklahoma Historical Society; 23, Archives and Manuscripts Division of the Oklahoma Historical Society; 24, The Bettmann Archive; 25, Archives and Manuscripts Division of the Oklahoma Historical Society; 26, ©Pat Wadecki/**Root Resources**; 27, ©**Tom Dietrich**; 28, David Ball/**Tony Stone Images, Inc.**; 29 (both pictures), Oklahoma Tourism photo by Fred W. Marvel; 30 (left), ©**Joan Dunlop**; 30 (right), ©Pat Wadecki/**Root Resources**; 31, ©Pat Wadecki/**Root Resources**; 32-33, ©Pat Wadecki/**Root Resources**; 34, Oklahoma Tourism Photo by Fred W. Marvel; 35, Oklahoma Tourism Photo by Fred W. Marvel; 36, ©Pat Wadecki/**Root Resources**; 37, ©H. Abernathy/**H. Armstrong Roberts**; 38, ©Martin Rogers/**Tony Stone Images, Inc.**; 39 (top), ©**Joan Dunlop**; 39 (bottom), ©Pat Wadecki/**Root Resources**; 40 (top), ©Wendell Metzen/**H. Armstrong Roberts**; 40 (bottom), Matt Bradley/**Tom Stack & Associates**; 41, ©David Ball/**Tony Stone Images, Inc.**; 42, ©**James P. Rowan**; 43, Oklahoma Tourism Photo by Fred W. Marvel; 44, Oklahoma Tourism Photo by Fred W. Marvel; 45 (both pictures), Oklahoma Tourism Photo by Fred W. Marvel; 46, Courtesy Will Rogers Memorial and Birthplace; 47, AP/**Wide World Photos**; 48, The Bettmann Archive; 49, AP/**Wide World Photos**; 50, AP/**Wide World Photos**; 51 (both pictures), AP/**Wideworld Photos**; 52 (top), UPI/**Bettmann**; 52 (bottom), **AP/Wide World Photos**; 53, AP/**Wide World Photos**; 54 (top), **Western History Collections, University of Oklahoma Library**; 54 (bottom), **Courtesy of Miracle-Gro Plant Food**; 55, Photograph property of *The Daily Oklahoman*; 56 (top), Courtesy Flag Research Center, Winchester, Massachusetts 01890; 56 (middle), ©R. C. Simpson/**Tom Stack & Associates**; 56 (bottom), ©Stan Osolinski/**Dembinsky Photo Assoc.**; 57 (top), ©John Kohout/**Root Resources**; 57 (middle), ©Thomas Kitchin/**Tom Stack & Associates**; 57 (bottom), *Outdoor Oklahoma*; 58, Oklahoma Tourism Photo by Fred W. Marvel; 60-61, Tom Dunnington; back cover, ©**Tom Till**

INDEX

Page numbers in boldface type indicate illustrations.

ABOUT THE AUTHOR

Dennis and Judith Fradin have coauthored several books in the From Sea to Shining Sea series. The Fradins both graduated from Northwestern University in 1967. Dennis has been a professional writer for twenty years, and has published 150 books. His works for Childrens Press include the Young People's Stories of Our States series, the Disaster! series, and the Thirteen Colonies series. Judith earned her M.A. in literature from Northwestern University and taught high-school and college English for many years. The Fradins, who are the parents of Anthony, Diana, and Michael, live in Evanston, Illinois.